A LATTE WITH LIFE

DHAWAN

For Mom, Dad, my dearest Friends and Her... :P

Contents

Preface

They say several epiphanies hit you throughout life. But my life was… let's say spice-less.
I had no girlfriends or even many friends and had no such bewildering experiences to write something as deep and insightful as poetry. Then life hit me with a turning point… a rock bottom.

I had a magical reunion with my all time crush! She's amazing and we hung out for a while until…
I suffered hypertension and lost both my kidneys… I was alone and depressed. Scared of the future. Lost my dream job. Hope. And perhaps I lost her too.

I then decided to gather myself and accept life as is. Finally took the time to finish My first book "Voh! - a spiritual perspective" which will get published later this year.

And meanwhile the poet in me woke up and I realized the power and magic of it. Poetry is enchanting and inspiring and I hope mine gives you an experience worth reading and sharing while you enjoy that delicious latte with life!

1. Another Latte with You

The silky side burns by your ear,
Flowed flawlessly down your cheek…
As smooth as your voice dwelled in my heart.

And then I'd turn my eyes back on the road,
As I drove with you by my side…
For another cup of latte.

Winters felt warmer with you,
I hope you felt it too…
We were so different, yet so alike,
Our union was crazy but it just felt right.

But then you disappeared,
Did it all end?
Now alone I steered,
Did I lose a friend?

I 'am scared of loosing you,
Do you feel it too?
but yes I will…
Still…
Wait for another latte with you.

2. The Clay Lamp

A warm clay lamp,
Playing with it's own shadow,
wiggles as it talks to me.

3. Picturesque

A vast panorama,
Dew blushing on the greens,
Gargantuan mountains along the edge,
It's a picturesque scene.

There's an old wooden fence,
And fragrant winds flow…
A distant flute,
With a gentle blow.

Look! a leaf flew by,
Swirling in the ember sky,
And lands in a silent puddle…
Giving it a tender cuddle.
And now comes the shepherd,
Marching with his sheep,
Do you see the light…
In his eyes so deep?

By the fence, look at her stand,
Old blue Jeans and a book in hand…
Freckled cheek and a dinky bun,
Is she sun kissed or kissing the sun?

4. Her Eyes

Big wondrous eyes,
Guarded with lush black lining,
Hide fathomless mysteries!

5. I Wonder!

I looked up and wondered…
if life was a dream…
and then I woke up.

I looked up and wondered…
if an artist sat above…
and then I learned to paint.

I looked up and wondered…
if only I could see…
and then I saw… it was me.

6. Her Letter

A crumbled letter,
Of love and forgiveness,
Rests under a dried rose.

7. महफ़िल

ख़यालों की महफ़िल में एक ख़याल तुम्हारा भी है,
बस उसी से गुफ़्तगू कर लेता हूँ...
और एक महफ़िल सी लग जाती है।

हाज़रीन-ए-महफ़िल गिला करते हैं,
कि उन्हें तुम्हारे लिए बेगाना कर दिया...
और चले जाते हैं हमें कुरबत में छोड़ कर।

फिर वही ख़ामोशी घेर लेती है हमें,
वही उल्फ़त भरे लम्हे...
उन लम्हों में ठहेर जाने का दिल करता है।

डरता हूँ कहीं धुंधला ना जाए चेहरा तुम्हारा,
खो ना दूँ तुम्हें दोबारा...
इस चेहरे के नूर में झूल जाता हूँ,
तुम एक ख़याल हो ये भूल जाता हूँ।

तुम कहती हो मैं ही क्यूँ?
क्या कोई और नज़र नहीं आता?
कैसे कहूँ जहाँ तुम ना हो,
उस महफ़िल में मैं नहीं जाता।

8. Her Feet

She silently raised her jeans…
And pointed at her new anklet,
Just above the breath-taking black thread.

9. Harshu's Hustle

Harshu had no clue,
Where the hell was his left shoe?
Hot breakfast ready on his plate,
But the 7th grader was running late.

Mom found the shoe under a table,
While Harshu got tangled in a cable!
Cried! the little sister, still hungry for more,
ting-tong! there was someone on the door.

Dad rushed to open it,
Harshu broke his geometry kit,
Shit!
The pointy compass fell on him,
And he got a wounding zit!

Harshu's bag was still a mess,
The inkpot then fell on his dress!
Outside the door the conductor stood,
But how could?
Oh no! it was seven already,
There was no time to be steady!

He ran and buckled on the way,
coz the driver could not stay,
His mother although had a hunch,
Of course!
Harshu left hungry and forgot his lunch!

10. Her Hair

A feather falls on her lustrous hair...
And slides along the silken curves,
All the way down to her waist.

11. Eleven Eleven

T'was eleven eleven,
so I prayed to the heavens...
for another chance,
to dance...
To the music I didn't hear before,
and I dint wanna fear no more...
I knew there'll be an open door,
for me...
to be free.

Then I was on the other side,
Browsing oceans far and wide...
Now a lion roared inside!
It said…
Conquer!!
Fear, Doubt and Guilt,
the rigid walls I had built...
were shattering!
Now I was with me,
Could feel the joy and glee…
I hope all luck turns my way,
But that's a wish for another day.

12. Her Hands

Her soft little hands…
Quiver as I gently touch them,
And teach her chopsticks.

13. Scars

Do you see my scars?
They aren't buried so deep.
Don't be disguised by the smile,
Behind which I weep.

Did you really have to go?
So sudden like this...
I'm sorry I dint take it slow...
I had no time to miss.

Knock knock! who's there?
Someone who loved and cared,
Why'd the door never open wide?
Were you even there on the other side?

Do you wanna try again?
For I have been through a lot,
My heart is lonely and in pain,
My heart is all I've got.

14. Her Lips

Sun flares touch her tender lips,
And she twitches them close…
But I keep looking.

15. Spiders

An eight legged monster
creeps in my room,
Scared to death I wonder...
where the hell's my broom!

My body begins to shiver
while my soul inside screams,
I'm watching it quiver
just like in my dreams!

I don't like spiders,
Not one bit!
They scare the hell out of me,
I know they've got some wit.
I feel the twitch,
And the constant itch,
Scarier than death,
Speaking of which...

Once I smashed a spider,
And flushed away its body,
But one of its broken legs...
Kept moving in my lobby!!!

When I see a spider...
anywhere near my bed,
I don't even move an inch,
even if I want it dead.

I get nightmares in day,
If I see one across the hall,
I wish I was a lizard,
and swallow them all!

16. Her Swirls

Her swirls get heavy in the rain...
and stick to her cheek,
slightly brushing her lips.

17. The Play

I decided to create,
an illusion so immersive,
a play so wonderful,
that I could experience
myself...
to the fullest.
Then a part of me split into pieces,
each piece glorious,
and I told them all to play.
Now my pieces danced in glee,
but each one knew...
it was a tiny part of me.
So before I let them go,
I covered each one with Ego!
Now each piece had an individuality,
a unique personality...
and now I could
look at the worlds I created
through their eyes.

They went into the world...
of dualities,
experiencing their own realities.

A place of day and night,
of days dark and bright,
of things big and small,
of people short and tall.
Life was a swirling tide...
a roller coaster ride,
so exciting!

But then ego took over
and my pieces forgot me.
I know they're having fun,
but it's time to return...
back home
be free and merge back into me,
before I create another play.

18. Blue

She was wearing blue...
just as I saw her in my dreams,
bewitching all my senses.

19. Rainbows

I don't see rainbows in the rain,
there is something blocking them,
oh! how I've missed catching them.
Yet when the clouds rumble,
I wait for them...
for the colors to just appear,
just once.
But I fear...
loosing this moment.

And then I am surrounded...
by dark dense clouds,
waiting for the sky to clear
and fresh dew to appear.
Longing for another day,
feels as dry as autumn,
coz I've hit the rock bottom.

20. Tide

She came like a silent tide,
I had my arms opened wide
and then it disappeared.

21. Turtle Doves

Two white turtle doves,
Kiss on a ledge and fly away,
Leaving behind a fragrant feather.

9 798887 725413

Printed by Libri Plureos GmbH in Hamburg,
Germany